Effective Interpersonal Relationships

D1604621

Effective Interpersonal Relationships

ROBERT W. LUCAS

Business Skills Express Series

IRWIN
Professional Publishing

MIRROR PRESS

Burr Ridge, Illinois
New York, New York
Boston, Massachusetts

IRWIN
Concerned About Our Environment

In recognition of the fact that our company is a large end-user of fragile yet replenishable resources, we at IRWIN can assure you that every effort is made to meet or exceed Environmental Protection Agency (EPA) recommendations and requirements for a "greener" workplace.

To preserve these natural assets, a number of environmental policies, both companywide and department-specific, have been implemented. From the use of 50% recycled paper in our textbooks to the printing of promotional materials with recycled stock and soy inks to our office paper recycling program, we are committed to reducing waste and replacing environmentally unsafe products with safer alternatives.

This publication is designed to provide accurate and authoritative information in regard to the subject matter covered. It is sold with the understanding that neither the author or the publisher is engaged in rendering legal, accounting, or other professional service. If legal advice or other expert assistance is required, the services of a competent professional person should be sought.

From a Declaration of Principles jointly adopted by a Committee of the American Bar Association and a Committee of Publishers.

Mirror Press:	David R. Helmstadter
	Carla F. Tishler
Editor-in-chief:	Jeffrey A. Krames
Project editor:	Karen J. Nelson
Production manager:	Jon Christopher
Designer:	Heidi J. Baughman
Art manager:	Kim Meriwether
Art studio:	Electra Graphics
Compositor:	Alexander Graphics, Inc.
Typeface:	12/14 Criterion Book
Printer:	Malloy Lithographing, Inc.

Library of Congress Cataloging-in-Publication Data

Lucas, Robert W.
  Effective interpersonal relationships / Robert W. Lucas.
    p.   cm. — (Business skills express Series)
  ISBN 0-7863-0255-0
  1. Psychology, Industrial.   2. Interpersonal relations.
  3. Communication in management.   I. Title.   II. Series.
  HF5548.8.L684   1994
  650.1'3—dc20   93–48220

Printed in the United States of America
1 2 3 4 5 6 7 8 9 0 ML 1 0 9 8 7 6 5 4

ABOUT THE AUTHOR

Robert William Lucas is the training manager at the national office of the American Automobile Association in Heathrow, Florida. He has extensive experience in the training, development, and management fields. For the past 20 years, he has conducted training in profit, nonprofit, not-for-profit, military, government, consulting, and volunteer environments. His areas of expertise include management and training program development, interpersonal communication, adult learning, customer service and employee development. Bob has served on the Board of Directors for the Metropolitan Chapter of the American Society for Training and Development in Washington, D.C. and in Orlando, Florida, where he is currently president-elect. Additionally, Bob has given presentations to various local and national groups and organizations, serves on a variety of product advisory committees for several national organizations, and is an adjunct faculty member at several Orlando area colleges.

ABOUT IRWIN PROFESSIONAL PUBLISHING

Irwin Professional Publishing is the nation's premier publisher of business books. As a Times Mirror company, we work closely with Times Mirror training organizations, including Zenger-Miller, Inc., Learning International, Inc., and Kaset International to serve the training needs of business and industry.

About the Business Skills Express Series

This expanding series of authoritative, concise, and fast-paced books delivers high-quality training on key business topics at a remarkably affordable cost. The series will help managers, supervisors, and frontline personnel in organizations of all sizes and types hone their business skills while enhancing job performance and career satisfaction.

Business Skills Express books are ideal for employee seminars, independent self-study, on-the-job training, and classroom-based instruction. Express books are also convenient-to-use references at work.

PREFACE

Every day you come into contact with a variety of people in the workplace: employees, peers, your supervisor, customers, and vendors. In each of these contacts, both you and the other person walk away with an opinion about the encounter. Whether your encounter will be a success or a failure depends in part on the strength of your interpersonal skills.

The number of supervisors and managers who have failed in the performance of their jobs and in their personal relationships due to poor interpersonal skills is not known. What is known is that many supervisors and managers take their interpersonal skills, or lack of them, for granted as they go through their daily workplace routines. You should not take yours for granted. As you move toward the 21st century, competition for your job will become more intense. To remain competitive and to position yourself as an asset to your organization and customers, you must develop and strengthen your people skills.

This book was written to stimulate your thought, test your knowledge, and provide tools for developing, refining, and building your interpersonal skills. Each chapter begins with a scenario designed to start you thinking about the material that follows in the chapter. As you proceed through this book, personalize it by highlighting key points, responding to the activities or questions, and making notes for future reference.

Robert W. Lucas

CONTENTS

Self-Assessment

Your ability to communicate and interact freely with others often affects the way others deal with you. This self-assessment will help you identify areas on which you may want to focus as you go through this book. Select the response that you feel best describes you in each situation presented and put the number of that selection before the statement.

Note: Since your image of yourself often differs from the one others have of you, make copies of this survey before completing it. Once you have rated yourself, distribute the copies to employees and co-workers who are familiar with your style in the workplace and ask them to rate you. Compare all of the results and develop an action plan to improve your skills.

KEY: 1 = Rarely   2 = Sometimes   3 = Frequently   4 = Usually   5 = Always

_____   **1.** I consciously strive for open two-way communication with my employees, peers, and supervisor.

_____   **2.** I use a structured procedure for giving feedback to others, and I give feedback on a regular basis.

_____   **3.** I think about the vocal cues I use when communicating with others, and I send only positive messages.

_____   **4.** When preparing for a meeting, I consciously think of the impact that my appearance will have on the other person and adjust accordingly.

_____   **5.** I think of the ultimate impact of my actions, or inactions, on relationships with others and do only things that encourage teamwork and cooperation.

_____   **6.** To get the most from conversations, I use my listening skills and focus intently during all exchanges.

_____   **7.** I think about each employee situation I encounter and select the management style best suited to encourage success.

_____   **8.** I use knowledge about different personality styles to help in relationships with others and select the best approach for dealing with each individual.

_____   **9.** I focus on limiting personal biases when interacting with others and treat everyone equally.

_____   **10.** Whenever conflict arises, I initiate appropriate action immediately to restore cooperation and teamwork.

Scoring

No matter what your score, this book will help you to acquire new skills and to strengthen the positive ones you already have. Your score will give you an indication of how far you need to go to achieve lasting success in your interpersonal relationships.

45–50	Excellent. Your relationships are probably strong.
40–44	Good job. Continue your efforts.
30–39	Fair effort. Stay focused on the positive.
20–29	Room for improvement. Get some personal feedback from others to help you improve.
Below 20	Evaluate your efforts. Something is missing.

---

1 | Building Interpersonal Relationships through Trust

This chapter will help you to:

- Identify a variety of strategies for building trust.
- Select an approach to building trust that will ensure success.
- Recognize the factors that affect trust in your relationships with others.

Recently promoted and ready to dive into her new career assignment as supervisor of the midnight shift, police sergeant Brittney Adamson held her first roll call. As she made the announcements for the evening, several of her former peers heckled her from the rear of the room. This was frustrating and a bit annoying, but she ignored them.

Prior to Brittney's promotion, she had enjoyed an amiable relationship with members of her team and with departmental supervisors. Now that she has been moved into a new role, she is a bit anxious about dealing with these same people and is unsure how she should approach them. It seems that even some of her new peers doubt her abilities. ■

■ Questions to Consider

1. Why do you think Brittney's former peers are acting in the manner described?

_____

_____

2. How can Brittney most effectively settle into her new relationship roles with her former peers? With her new peers?

_____

_____

_____

3. What are some possible strategies that Brittney can use to deal effectively with her former peers without alienating them?

_____

_____

_____

THE BASIS FOR TRUST

When you are promoted to a supervisory or managerial role, one of your biggest challenges is gaining the trust of people who were once your peers. Too often promotions to higher levels occur because of an individual's technical expertise, not because of strong interpersonal skills. Training, coaching, and support are often inadequate to prepare for new responsibilities and assignments. From a trust-building standpoint, you must remember that your key responsibility as a supervisor is to your people. They are the vehicle through which you succeed or fail. Addressing their needs should be your primary goal.

To help your employees perform at their peak level, you must establish a level of trust with them. Only with their trust and cooperation can you and your organization reach established goals. You must work quickly and consciously to gain cooperation and obtain a commitment to perform at or above established levels. As the supervisor-employee relationship matures, you must continue to conduct "reality checks" by gathering feedback to stay in tune with your employees.

STRATEGIES FOR BUILDING TRUST

As a supervisor, you must earn trust. Most people will have confidence in you and will expect you to be able to perform your job simply because you are the supervisor. It is up to you to demonstrate that you are capable of doing the job. Here are some strategies for helping to gain the trust of others.

- **Communicate effectively and convincingly.** If you cannot communicate your knowledge to others, you will not be effective in convincing them to believe you. You must provide your employees more than simple facts and figures. Project your feelings as you communicate; this will make you appear more human and approachable.

- **Demonstrate that you are capable.** Obviously, your superior believed you had the basic qualifications to do your job or you would not have been promoted. It is up to you to show that this belief was well founded. You need to perform in a manner that convinces others that they can depend on you to get the job done.

- **Display concern for others.** Emphasize helping others rather than yourself. Being available and willing to assist when necessary shows that you have the goodwill of others in mind.

- **Be fair.** Nothing will turn others against you faster than treating your subordinates inconsistently. Assist, reward, coach, counsel, and punish equitably to avoid problems and resentment.

- **Admit when you are wrong and when you do not know.** People generally warm up to those who appear human. To err or to not have all the answers is human. You often can win people over by appealing to them for help. But do so in a sincere manner, not just to make them feel needed. They may read the latter as paternalism and could become offended.

- **Foster a "team player" image.** Be a part of the team and encourage others to do the same. Something as simple as coordinating a team meeting or an after work get-together can go a long way.

1

■ **Trust others.** By showing that you trust others, you can gain their trust in return. One way to demonstrate your trust is to share information freely and quickly. If you or someone higher makes a decision that affects others and it is not confidential or damaging, pass the information on to others.

APPROACHES TO TRUST BUILDING

Relationships and trust levels are direct spin-offs of the climate you set or allow to exist in the workplace. Think about your own workplace environment. Are employees happy, effective, efficient, communicating openly, and willing to do more than their share? Or is there a lot of complaining, rumors, low productivity, poor morale, and reluctance to voluntarily pitch in when needed? As a leader, people look to you to set the example or benchmark for others to follow. Several approaches can be used to establish a benchmark for trust in the workplace. Unfortunately, not all are positive. The following are three common approaches along with potential outcomes. Examine and match them to your relationships in the workplace. If you find that many outcomes you typically encounter are negative, you may want to try an alternative approach.

Approach	Demonstrated Through	Potential Outcomes
Defensive	■ Failure to share information.	Two-way communication is stifled.
	■ Lack of interaction with others.	Others avoid contact with you.
	■ Reluctance to solicit help when needed.	Others may doubt your competence or ability.
	■ Judging performance critically or unfairly.	Animosity lowers productivity, self-esteem and respect for you.
	■ Strictly "business only" or facts only interactions (by the book).	Perception of your lack of caring or sensitivity.
	■ Being condescending to others.	Lowered cooperation and lack of respect for you.
	■ Actual or perceived manipulation of others.	Resentment, animosity, or a desire to "get even."

Approach	Demonstrated Through	Potential Outcomes
Supportive	• Giving regular feedback and credit for accomplishments.	Raised self-esteem for others.
	• Warm and friendly attitude.	Positive interactions with others.
	• Honest, open communication.	Mutual trust and sharing.
	• Applauding initiative and creativity.	Future repeated positive behavior.
	• Treating employees as equals.	Increased respect and cooperation.
	• Being available, but not forcing assistance on others.	Appreciation, respect, and feeling of having a "safety net," if needed.
Collaborative	• Sharing information fully.	Ongoing, open exchange of information.
	• Providing opportunities to participate.	Increased self-esteem, productivity, and trust.
	• Distributing authority freely and equitably.	Raised perceptions of being part of the team and being important.
	• Reciprocating cooperation or simply saying "thank you."	Ongoing, increased interaction.
	• Self-disclosure.	A view of you as human, leading others to understand and communicate better with you and to self-disclose more freely themselves.
	• Working with others to develop or accomplish goals.	Camaraderie or feelings of team develop.
	• Encouraging creativity and risk taking.	Increased efficiency and productivity and stimulated effectiveness.

Supervisors approach trust building in a variety of ways.

1

Personal Reflection

Take a few minutes to think of a time when you have had or have witnessed an encounter in which someone was not trusted. Answer these questions about that situation.

1. What were some of the person's actions, or inactions, that created the lack of trust?

   _____

   _____

   _____

2. How could the person have changed others' perceptions of him or her and have improved the relationship?

   _____

   _____

   _____

Based on your responses to this activity, do a quick self-analysis to ensure that you are not demonstrating the same behaviors that you dislike in others.

FACTORS AFFECTING TRUST

Many things that you do have an effect on whether people trust you. Here are some possibilities.

- **Decision making.** The manner in which you make or fail to make decisions sends a powerful message about your commitment to the organization, to your team members, and to others around you. Before making a decision, determine desired outcomes, gather and analyze facts, consider alternatives and possible results, and consult with others, if necessary.

- **Timing.** Develop relationships with employees, peers, and your supervisor quickly. If you typically find yourself saying, "I'll coach, call, or have lunch with them later," you may find it difficult to regain lost opportunities to develop a strong interpersonal relationship because you postponed contact.

- **Personal characteristics.** Many aspects of your personality affect the way others view you:

  - Communication style
  - Beliefs
  - Honesty
  - Initiative
  - Ability to follow through
  - Values
  - Sincerity
  - Truthfulness
  - Devotion
  - Fairness

It is your responsibility to decide how you want to be perceived and work toward meeting that vision.

- **Demeanor.** The way in which you approach others (direct/indirect/both) can determine their response or reaction to you. By knowing about personality style preferences for yourself and others, you can often avoid conflicts or misunderstandings. This knowledge can be gained through personality-style profile questionnaires (e.g., Performax, Myers-Briggs). It is especially effective to know the results of another person's style profile when interacting with him or her. This allows you to address their preferences or tendencies.

1

- **Feedback.** Your ability, desire, and skill in delivering regular, timely, and honest feedback is crucial in building trust with others. By avoiding game playing or the perception that you either do not care or are a "yes" person, you stimulate others' confidence in you.

- **Environment.** If you create or foster an environment that stifles creativity, achievement, rewards, and communication, you will negatively impact morale, self-esteem, efficiency, and productivity.

Expanding on What You Have Learned

Take a few minutes to reflect on some of the ideas covered in this chapter; then answer these questions.

1. Think about your own personality and preferences. What are your strengths? What are your weaknesses?

   _____

   _____

   _____

2. What actions are you currently doing in the workplace that could inhibit building trust with others?

   _____

   _____

   _____

3. If you are currently experiencing or were to experience a breakdown in trust with one of your employees or co-workers, what would you do to remedy it? What if the breakdown were with your supervisor?

   _____

   _____

   _____

Chapter 1 Checkpoints

Trust is vital in getting your job done and building successful interpersonal relationships with others. When interacting with others, remember to:

✓ Show concern and help others.

✓ Communicate openly.

✓ Be consistent and fair with others.

✓ Work with others to ensure your mutual success as well as the success of your team and organization.

✓ Choose a trust-building approach that will result in positive outcomes.

✓ Stay aware of the factors that affect trust and work toward using them effectively.

2 | Communicating for Effectiveness

This chapter will help you to:

- Recognize the importance of interpersonal communication in developing and maintaining relationships.
- Utilize guidelines for effective interpersonal communication to help foster stronger interactions with others.
- Identify key elements of the two-way communication process.
- Adapt your communication style to interact more effectively in a variety of situations.
- Remove barriers to communication.
- Develop the characteristics of an influential supervisor.
- Initiate and strengthen your ability to network effectively.

Timothy O'Connor, a reproduction department manager, had just arrived at work when Dawn Philips came into his office. She was visibly upset as she began to speak. "Tim, I've had all I can take. You've got to do something about the workload around here. I didn't get out of here until 9 o'clock last night and I've already been in for an hour this morning. My husband and kids don't even recognize me anymore!"

Tim knew things had been hectic in Dawn's area, but he had no idea that they had reached this level. "You look really upset Dawn, and that concerns me. Please tell me in detail what's going on and how I can help."

2

Dawn responded, "I've told you before, Tim, that I've got to have more people or we've got to start contracting work to outside printers. We have increased our output by 32 percent in the past six months and still don't have the help you promised."

"I know," Tim countered. "Your team has really been doing a great job lately, and I appreciate the results. I've been meaning to tell you for the past two weeks that the new employee position was approved by Human Resources and we start recruiting next week."

"That's great, but why didn't you tell me sooner? Do you realize that I was ready to turn in my resignation today?"

Tim was shocked. "I had no idea things were that serious, Dawn. If I lost you, I'd really be in a mess; you're the best supervisor I've got." He continued, "Let's schedule some time for catching up on what's going on and develop a plan of action for getting you that help you need. Then I want to discuss how we got to this point and make sure that it never happens again. I really value you and don't want to lose you to a competitor."

Smiling, Dawn replied, "It's a deal. When would you like to get together?" ■

Questions to Consider

1. Based on this scenario, how well is Tim doing in communicating with his employees? Explain.

_____

_____

_____

2. Once Dawn identified her concerns to Tim, how well do you feel he handled the situation? Explain.

_____

_____

_____

3. What could Tim have done earlier to prevent the escalation that brought Dawn into his office?

_____

_____

_____

THE IMPORTANCE OF COMMUNICATION

Communication is the network through which you and others in the organization gather information from each other to effect goals. It permeates every aspect of your daily work life. As a supervisor, you must consciously be aware of your own communication style and look for various communication signals from your employees. People will show signs of frustration, stress, concern, or anger, often without confronting you with the underlying causes of their feelings. If you are not familiar with or do not recognize the various components of the communication process and how each affects the meaning of the messages delivered, you could face what Tim faced in the chapter-opening scenario.

Have you ever wondered why you are able to relate to and communicate so well with some people yet so poorly with others? Although there is no one answer to this question, by identifying basic guidelines for effective interpersonal communication, you may gain insights and be able to strengthen your ability to interact effectively.

2

GUIDELINES FOR EFFECTIVE INTERPERSONAL COMMUNICATION

The following actions can develop or strengthen your relationships with others. Several of these are analogous to the strategies for building trust outlined in Chapter 1.

- **Gather your thoughts and information before you initiate communication.** Failure to do so could leave the impression that you are disorganized or ill-prepared and not worth listening to.

- **Never approach someone to discuss a topic when you are angry or upset.** Anger can cloud your judgment and cause you to say things you do not mean or make mistakes that could cost you later. Always take time to cool down. Plan your approach logically; then take necessary action.

- **Be prepared to give immediate, specific, and honest feedback in any interaction.** Unless you tell people openly how you feel or what you need them to know, they can only guess—causing much confusion, resentment, and failure.

- **Realize that if a message is important enough for someone to verbalize, it is probably important to him or her.** Even if someone tells you that an issue is "no big deal," if he or she brought it up in the first place, you need to address it and come to a resolution to prevent it from escalating.

- **Take time to send messages carefully and accurately to avoid misinterpretation.** As you may have heard, "Haste makes waste," and if you are like most supervisors, you do not have an abundance of extra time to correct problems created by not handling something correctly in the first place.

- **Avoid trying to intimidate or pressure someone into action.** This will result only in resentment and frustration while damaging your relationship.

- **Strive for consistency in dealing with others.** This can go a long way to reduce employee stress and apprehension. Treating others fairly and equitably sends a message that you are trustworthy and concerned about others.

- **Follow through on all commitments.** If you find yourself unable to perform or deliver as promised, inform those people affected immediately.

- **Admit your mistakes or take the blame when you create problems.** Failure to do so could damage your credibility.

- **Be ready to assist others.** Helping others will gain you supporters while increasing your popularity and effectiveness.

- **Provide credit and praise when others are responsible for successes.** Most people want and need recognition. Giving it goes a long way to prove that you are supportive of others.

- **Never criticize others in front of someone.** As a rule of thumb, follow the adage "Praise in public, criticize in private." Failure to remember this could cause a loss of loyalty, trust, and respect.

- **Respect confidences when others share information with you.** Never pass on information entrusted to you. If you do pass it on, it may be the last information you ever get from that person, and your reputation as a trustworthy individual may suffer severely.

- **Judge people based on factors over which they have control, not on ones over which they do not (race, sex, age, ethnicity, or physical and mental characteristics).** Focusing on uncontrollable characteristics is both unfair and not very smart. It could also violate anti-discrimination laws.

A MODEL FOR TWO-WAY COMMUNICATION

As you have seen, your ability to do your job effectively as a supervisor hinges on how well you communicate with others. True two-way communication can occur only when both parties are committed to the purpose of the interaction. As a supervisor, it is to your advantage to ensure that in all exchanges with employees, peers, your supervisor, customers, vendors, or whomever, you follow the basic guidelines of interpersonal communication outlined earlier. It is also important that you understand the variables involved in effective two-way communication.

Numerous communication models are available to explain what takes place during communication with other people. The following interpersonal communication model contains key elements that you should recognize and focus on during interactions with others. The factors (described on page 17) are shown in the model below.

Interpersonal Communication Model

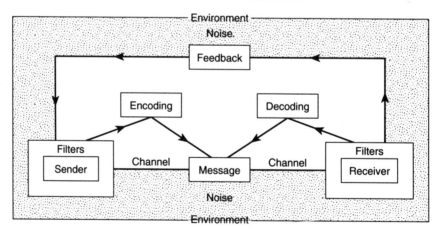

Communication Model Factors

- **Environment.** The environment in which you send or receive messages affects how effective your communication is.

- **Sender.** You take on the role of sender as you initiate a message or interaction with someone else.

- **Receiver.** Initially, you serve as the recipient of the sender's message; however, once you return feedback, you switch to the sender role.

- **Message.** The message is the idea or concept that you wish to convey.

- **Channel.** The method or conduit you choose to transmit your message (over the phone, in person, by fax, by computer modem, or by other means).

- **Encoding.** Encoding occurs as you evaluate what must be done to effectively put the message into a format that the recipient of your message will understand (language, symbols, and gestures are a few options). Failing to correctly determine your receiver's ability to decode your message could lead to confusion or misunderstanding.

- **Decoding.** Decoding occurs as you convert the messages you receive back into familiar ideas and interpret or assign meaning. Depending on how well the sender encoded the message or whether or not your filters interfere, the message you receive may not be the one the sender intended.

- **Feedback.** Unless a response is given to messages received, you have no way to determine if your intended message was received. Feedback is one of the most crucial elements of the two-way communication process. Without it, you have a monologue.

- **Filters.** Filters are factors that distort or affect the messages you receive. They include, among others, your attitude, interests, biases, expectations, education, beliefs, and values.

- **Noise.** Noises are any physiological or psychological factors (your physical characteristics, lack of attention, message clarity, loudness of message, or environmental factors) that interfere with accurate reception of information.

2

BARRIERS TO EFFECTIVE COMMUNICATION

Many things can inhibit your ability to send and receive messages effectively. To achieve maximum efficiency in interpersonal communication, you should strive to reduce the following barriers:

- **Unfamiliarity with technology.** Confusion, misunderstanding, or failure to receive messages could result if you are unaccustomed to the technology used to transmit a message (technical features of a telephone, fax, or PC modem).

- **Preconceived ideas.** By assuming that you know the answer or point the person is trying to make without first getting all the facts or a complete message, you are likely to misinterpret the sender's meaning.

- **Emotions.** When your emotions are raised so high that you become angry, upset, stressed, or otherwise excited, you are likely to misinterpret information received.

- **Evaluation of sender.** When you focus on forming an opinion of the sender, you may inhibit your ability to make an unbiased interpretation of messages received.

- **Distractions.** By making a conscious effort to screen out factors that may distort the incoming message or distract you, your effectiveness can increase.

- **Semantics.** Certain words or phrases can send inappropriate or differing meanings. Avoid jargon, inflammatory language, technical terms, or other language that may confuse your intended message receiver.

- **Inconsistency between verbal and nonverbal cues.** To avoid confusion, use gestures and other nonverbal cues that match your verbal message. Avoid signals that might send dual messages.

- **Distrust.** Distrust leads directly to failure. The trust factor is a key determinant to whether you are successful in interactions with others.

CHARACTERISTICS OF INFLUENTIAL SUPERVISORS

Being a good communicator is vital in helping you gain status, influence, power, and increased effectiveness when working with others. Used properly, communication can help you get the results you want and need as a supervisor. Some of the characteristics you need to possess in order to develop and maintain relationships with others include the following:

- **Ability to set goals.** By setting attainable goals and consistently working toward them, you demonstrate decisiveness, dependability, and commitment.

- **Ability to stimulate decisiveness.** You will often find yourself encouraging or in some cases pushing others to attain their goals. By projecting a confident and decisive air, you will bolster others' confidence in you.

- **Ability to create visions in yourself and others.** In a competitive environment, only the strong survive. The strong are the visionaries who can nurture an idea into a full-fledged plan of action and spur on others to fulfill the plan.

- **Ability to adapt.** Change is inevitable on a daily basis. As organizations evolve, develop, and jockey for position, you must adapt to stay on top.

- **Ability to deal with diversity.** Diversity in a multitude of shapes and descriptions abounds in the workplace. As a supervisor, you must adapt to and manage it.

- **Ability to push others to peak levels.** Your team members look to you to lead, set the example, and provide a vehicle for their ultimate success. Failure to understand this and how to get the most from others could prove disastrous.

2

- **Ability to persuade others.** You may be the best visionary, motivator, and decision maker in your organization. Unless you can sell others on your ideas, however, you may limit your own success.

Take a few minutes to list the characteristics you have seen influential people exhibit.

_____

_____

_____

NETWORKING YOUR WAY TO SUCCESS

Networking is simply another means of communication. If you have ever heard the cliché "It's not what you know; it's who you know," you can appreciate the significance of personal networking. The ability to meet people and develop meaningful relationships is a major tool to help you to get your job done. You cannot possibly know all the answers or have all the skills needed to be successful in the workplace. You need other people to assist and support your efforts. That is where networking comes in. As you meet new people and learn their strengths, you are building a resource bank. When you need a certain skill or bit of information, you simply contact the appropriate person. You get needed help or advice, you look good in the eyes of others, and the job gets done more effectively and efficiently. Here are some basic rules to help with networking.

- **Smile—openly and regularly.** Let people know that you are friendly and approachable.

- **Target a variety of people.** Don't get into a habit of gathering with your co-workers or people you already know. When you attend training programs, meetings, or go to the cafeteria or a social event, sit with new people to expand your personal and professional network. Look for people who are not just like you (sex, race, job level, or age). Everyone has unique qualities and qualifications; find out what they are.

2

- **Mingle and get to know people.** You do not meet people by sitting by yourself in the lunch room, staying in your office all day, or isolating yourself in training programs and meetings. Go out of your way to meet and greet people.

- **Arrive early for meetings or training sessions.** This provides an excellent opportunity to get to know people over coffee or in an unstructured environment. Take the time during lunch or breaks to network instead of rushing to a phone or to your office to see how things are going. The office and work will be there when you return, but a networking opportunity might not present itself again.

- **Pass out business cards.** If your organization does not provide them, get business cards. It is a sound investment to have your own printed at the local business supply store or printer. Put your name, organization, title, phone number, and fax number (if applicable) on them. The cost is minimal, may be tax deductible, and will pay dividends in the future. Do not stop selling yourself just because you have a position. You may want to change jobs someday and a solid network can help. Carry cards with you wherever you go; you never know when a networking opportunity might arise (at the doctor's office, seminar, supermarket, library, holiday party).

- **Return all phone calls—even if you know that the caller is a vendor with whom you have no immediate business.** There may come a time when you will need a product or service for a project. It is far easier to go through your list of contacts than to start from scratch. Additionally, salespeople tend to have a very large network of their own that you may be able to tap.

There is no real mystique about networking. It is simply a matter of communicating care and making the effort to meet others.

2

Expanding on What You Have Learned

1. Can you adequately position yourself in your organization and develop a power base without learning to effectively communicate? Explain.

   _____

   _____

   _____

2. Successful leaders follow basic guidelines for developing strong interpersonal relationships with others. What are you currently doing to strengthen your relationships?

   _____

   _____

   _____

3. Review the barriers to communication covered in this chapter. What barriers do you create when communicating with others?

   _____

   _____

   _____

4. How can you eliminate the barriers you identified in question 3?

   _____

   _____

   _____

5. What steps can you take to become more influential in your workplace?

   _____

   _____

   _____

Chapter 2 Checkpoints

✓ Many personal factors affect your relationships with others. Be aware of them.

✓ For maximum effectiveness in two-way communication, you need a sender and a receiver who are both conscious of the other elements in the communication process.

✓ Calculated effort is needed to overcome the barriers to interpersonal communication.

✓ To gain influence with others, work to develop the characteristics outlined in this chapter.

✓ Take the time to network. It can pay big dividends later.

3 | Verbal Communication Skills

This chapter will help you to:

- Use your vocal qualities effectively to maximize message understanding.
- Realize the importance of choosing the right words when communicating.
- Recognize the need to build a powerful vocabulary.
- Identify and develop image-enhancing speech.
- Avoid words and phrases that interrupt interpersonal communication.

Meehir Vakharia has been working for 11 months for CenTech, a computer software development company in the Silicon Valley of California. He joined the company three months after graduating from a leading computer training program at the state university. Meehir is particularly proud of getting such a coveted position, especially since he has been in the United States for only two years. He goes out of his way to try to demonstrate his abilities and willingness to learn.

Yesterday afternoon before closing time, Jennifer Slader, Meehir's supervisor, stopped by his office briefly and instructed him to clean out the common work station and straighten the area before going home. Following Jennifer's instructions, Meehir nodded his understanding and went to handle the assignment.

3

The common area is often used by contract programmers hired to test new software and associated documentation before sending it for field testing. Upon arriving at the work station, Meehir discovered that there were quite a few old software diskettes and manuals on the table, floor, and nearby shelves. He dutifully set about cleaning and then went home.

This morning, Jennifer called Meehir into her office to ask what he had done with the documentation and diskettes from the work station. He replied, "I cleaned up as you instructed me. I threw all of the old material away as you said."

Jennifer felt the color drain from her face as she sank back into her chair as Meehir continued that in his country, when you "straighten up," you throw away everything on the floor.

Jennifer was dumfounded. Meehir had disposed of thousands of dollars in prototype program diskettes and manuals. She guessed that the total loss, with programming time figured in, was hundreds of thousands of dollars. ■

Questions to Consider

1. What are some of the issues in this scenario?

   _____

   _____

2. Think of a time when you were involved in a similar misunderstanding. Why did it occur?

   _____

   _____

3. What could Jennifer have done to prevent this incident?

_____

_____

As you saw in the communicating model in Chapter 2, encoding messages correctly is vital to understanding. Choosing the right language to communicate your thoughts can mean the ultimate success or failure of your message. In this case, Jennifer obviously did not consider potential language barriers.

3

As you interact with others in the workplace, you will encounter many situations in which you will have to select your words and actions carefully. Whether you are being politically sensitive, technically correct, or just trying to use good grammar, you must be conscious of multiple messages when you communicate. There are basically four potential types of messages sent whenever you communicate:

1. The message you want to send.

2. The message you thought you sent.

3. The message you actually sent.

4. The message the receiver understood.

With all these possibilities, it is no wonder that people in every organization complain about communication problems.

In a classic study on communication conducted by Albert Mehrabian[1], it was found that 38 percent of message meaning is derived from vocal qualities (speech rate, pitch, volume, and articulation) rather than from the spoken words. Nonverbal cues (face and body language) make up another

---

[1]Albert Mehrabian, "Communication without Words," *Psychology Today* 2 (September 1968), pp. 52–55.

3

55 percent. Interestingly, Mehrabian found that when the nonverbal behavior contradicts the verbal message, the meaning of the spoken words is altered and messages other than the ones intended are conveyed.

■ Communication Awareness

At your next opportunity, take a few minutes to walk around your workplace. As you pass various people, ask, "How are you?" or "How's it going?" Come back and answer these questions.

1. What messages did you get verbally?

   _____

   _____

2. What messages did you get nonverbally?

   _____

   _____

3. What body language did you note?

   _____

   _____

4. Were the verbal and nonverbal messages matched, or were different messages being relayed by each?

   _____

   _____

COMPONENTS OF VOCAL EXPRESSION

Vocal communication involves more than words. Here are some of its components.

■ **Rate.** The speed at which you deliver a message verbally is known as your *rate of speech*. The average adult in the business environment speaks at approximately 125–150 words per minute. Depending on the region or country in which the person was reared, the rate might vary. For instance, some people from rural areas speak at a somewhat slower rate than those from faster-paced urban areas. You should speak at a rate that is easily understood without losing your listener's interest or ability to decode your message.

■ **Volume.** How loudly or softly you speak is referred to as *volume.* To be effective, you must be heard without irritating others. If people continue to ask you to speak up or seem to be backing away as you speak, you may want to check your volume.

■ **Pitch.** Adjusting the highness or lowness of your vocal quality as you speak can add variety to your messages. Your pitch can add zest to your communication by showing enthusiasm, seriousness, or other emotions. It can also add vocal punctuation marks to your speech. For instance, think of how some peoples' voice pitch goes up at the end of their sentence when they are asking a question.

■ **Articulation.** The clarity with which you pronounce words says much about you and can help or hinder understanding your message. People often judge your social status, education level, confidence, motivation, and a variety of other factors based on how well you speak. For instance, if you tend to slur words (*didja, wouldja, hadda*) or drop word endings (*doin', gettin', bein'*), you could be viewed as lazy or even illiterate by some people.

Sentence Interpretation

To get an idea of how certain vocal components can affect message meaning, try repeating the following sentences, placing emphasis only on the highlighted words. You may find it helpful to tape-record the sentences and play them back afterward.

"*I* cannot believe you said that."

"I *cannot* believe you said that."

3

"I cannot *believe* you said that."

"I cannot believe *you* said that."

"I cannot believe you *said* that."

"I cannot believe you said *that*."

Notice that each version sends a different meaning based on the non-verbal change in vocal quality. This same effect occurs when various emotions come into play as you communicate verbally.

THE SIGNIFICANCE OF VOCABULARY

In past years, a solid vocabulary may not have been very important; however, as you move toward the 21st century, more people will be better educated and will expect you to be able to effectively communicate. Your inability to effectively exchange information could affect your ability to interact with others and could even affect your promotion potential.

Developing a sound vocabulary is not that difficult to do. Helpful resources include books, periodicals, college courses, audiotapes, dictionaries, and seminars.

Building a Power Vocabulary

To impress people with sophisticated or intellectual words or phrases, you may be tempted to use complicated words or phrases—DON'T! You will often confuse less-educated people and alert truly educated people of your inability to communicate effectively if you use the wrong words. Instead, strive for consistency and clarity.

Here is a list of commonly misused or overused words and phrases that you may hear in the workplace, along with some possible alternatives.

Common Language	Possible Alternatives
In regard to	About; concerning
At this point in time	Presently; now
On behalf of	For
In accordance with	With; by; following
In a number of cases	Some
On a few occasions	Occasionally
Deem	Think
In an effort to	To
Constitutes	Is; forms; makes up
In order to	To
In the event of	If
Solicit	Ask for
Validate	Confirm; check
Quid pro quo	Something in return for something
Along the lines of	Like
Apprise	Inform

3

IMAGE ENHANCING

Each cultural or social group has unique phrases, words, or symbols to communicate certain messages. Depending on the environment and people you find yourself dealing with, you may want to modify your vocabulary. Appropriate communication style with one person may not be with another. For example, language used with a relative or friend may not be appropriate with your supervisor or a customer.

If you have ever known someone who you felt was indecisive, weak, or simply uninteresting, you probably have known a poor communicator (among other things). Such people may display a lack of confidence, enthusiasm, or concern by the way they communicate verbally. See if you recognize any of these message patterns:

3

Language Used	Potential Message	Possible Alternative
"Gee whiz" or "Golly"	"I haven't expanded my vocabulary since the 1950s."	Eliminate
"Cool"	"I'm lost in the 60's."	Eliminate
"I don't care; whatever you think."	"Don't ask me for a decision or original idea; I *don't* care."	Make a decision.
"If it's not too much trouble . . ."	Intimidated; insecure	"Please . . ."
"Whatever comes down the pike . . ."	"I have no control; I lack confidence."	Develop a plan or strategy.
"The problem is . . ."	"I focus only on negatives."	"The issue is . . ."
"What I'd like to do . . ."	"I can't make up my mind"; intimidated.	Do it.
"I'll try . . ."	"I lack confidence."	"I'll do . . ."

Preferred Vocabulary

Customer service research[2] has led to the following preferred vocabulary choices. By following these lists' suggestions to use some words and avoid others, you'll increase favorable response to your messages.

Words/Phrases to Use	Words/Phrases to Avoid
Are you willing?	You have to . . .
How can it be corrected?	It's just a . . .
I apologize for . . .	I need (want) you to . . .
Will you?	This is the best (worst)
How can I help?	But . . .
However, . . .	You must . . .

[2] KASEL International (Tampa, FL, 1968).

Words/Phrases to Use	Words/Phrases to Avoid
What have you considered?	What's your problem?
I will; I am willing.	I'm sorry . . .
What do you want me to do?	I can't/You can't . . .
What are the options?	You are required . . .
I am able to . . .	It's necessary . . .
I understand.	It's our policy . . .
Here are some options . . .	Would you mind . . . ?
Which do you prefer?	You should/ought to . . .
I am unable . . .	I'll try . . .
I made a mistake.	Jargon of any type
What are the alternatives?	

VERBAL DISRUPTERS

Many people use verbal highlighters to emphasize their meaning or get feedback. Be cautious of using them inappropriately or excessively, since they can detract from your intended message and interfere with relationships. Often people will respond to these disrupters as they think you *want* them to reply. The following are some examples.

Disrupter	Potential Result
"You know?"	A response of "yes" from your listener with no true comprehension of your meaning.
"You know what I mean?"	Affirmative answers without true comprehension; feeling of resentment from your implication of their ignorance.
"Do you understand?"	Feelings that you don't believe they are intelligent enough to comprehend.
"Right?"	Feelings that you don't really want comprehension, but a "yes" response.
"Are you with me?"	Feelings that you believe they are not sharp enough to follow your meaning or communication.

▮ Expanding on What You Have Learned

Now that you have reviewed some of the factors that affect your verbal communication, take some time to answer these questions.

1. What are some personal communication areas you plan to examine to improve your interpersonal relationships?

   _____

   _____

2. Why do you think so much of a message's meaning is derived from nonverbal and vocal cues?

   _____

   _____

3. How can awareness of the importance of vocabulary work for your future success?

   _____

   _____

4. When delivering messages to others, how can you ensure that the message received is the one you intended?

   _____

   _____

Chapter 3 Checkpoints

Much of your time as a supervisor is spent communicating verbally with others. When sending messages, keep the following in mind:

✓ The majority of message meaning is derived from vocal qualities and nonverbal cues.

✓ Your vocabulary can send messages of strength or weakness; work to improve it.

✓ Examine your vocabulary to ensure that you are sending only clear, concise messages.

✓ Your professional image hinges on the way you communicate verbally. Eliminate weak, indecisive language.

✓ Select words and phrases that communicate a willingness to help or serve others.

✓ Watch out for verbal disrupters that can derail your message intent.

4 | The Role of Nonverbal Communication

This chapter will help you to:

- Define the role of nonverbal cues in interpersonal communication.
- Recognize nonverbal cues through which people send messages.
- Realize the importance of matching verbal and nonverbal cues when communicating.
- Select appropriate nonverbal cues to improve effectiveness when sending messages.

Stacy Connor sits across from Irene Hernandez, a customer service supervisor for Design Art, a mid-size graphic arts supplier based in Detroit, Michigan. Irene seems very serious and has said virtually nothing as she thumbs through paperwork.

Stacy has been with Design Art for six months and is about to receive her first performance appraisal. She is a bit apprehensive because she has been out sick for the past two days and feels that her absences could affect her performance rating. As she waits for Irene to break the silence, Stacy fidgets, crosses and uncrosses her legs, and can feel herself perspiring. She believes she has done a good job and needs a good rating to help her get a pay increase. Stacy is the sole provider for her chronically ill mother, who lives with her.

Irene finally shifts her attention from the papers to Stacy after several minutes. She smiles and begins, "I want you to know that I am very pleased with your work." She pauses, "But I cannot keep you in the layout section any longer." Stacy's heart sinks and she is visibly shaken as her mouth drops open. She almost bursts into tears, and then Irene continues, "You are too talented. I am recommending that you become the team leader for a special department being formed to support one of our major clients." Irene goes on, "Of course, with the added responsibility comes a pay increase. How does a 12 percent increase sound to you?"

Stacy is speechless. She smiles broadly, nods anxiously, and thanks Irene for her confidence and support. ∎

Questions to Consider

1. Based on Stacy's early nonverbal cues, what message might Irene have derived?

   _____

   _____

2. After viewing Stacy's nonverbal cues, could Irene have done anything to reduce obvious tension? Explain.

   _____

   _____

3. What thoughts were possibly on Stacy's mind based on Irene's initial nonverbal cues?

   _____

   _____

4. Did Irene's early nonverbal cues and her message match? Explain.

   _____

   _____

As the Mehrabian study (see Chapter 3) pointed out, most (55 percent) meaning from a message comes from nonverbal cues. With so much of your communication success riding on your ability to recognize and use nonverbal cues, it is worth taking some time to explore the issue.

Think about this statement: *It is impossible for you to "not communicate."* Do you agree or disagree? Explain.

_____

_____

_____

4

Everything you do sends a message: the way you sit, stand, look, move—everything. For that reason, you should consider methods to send only positive nonverbal signals that project an image of which you are proud. At the same time, you should work to improve your ability to identify and read others' nonverbal signals.

NONVERBAL COMMUNICATION PROBLEMS

Why should you use caution in placing emphasis on nonverbal cues received from others? Although you may potentially gather a lot of information through nonverbal cues from others, putting too much emphasis on them can lead to trouble. Many factors influence the messages being sent by others. The easiest way to prevent misinterpretation is to ask someone to clarify his or her nonverbal cues when you are unsure of their meaning.

The following are some factors that influence nonverbal messages:

• **Relationship to other cues.** Because nonverbal cues are often joined with other cues, you should be careful not to view them out of context. For example, you probably often get a nod of the head accompanied by a smile and "Good morning/afternoon" as you pass and greet another person in your office hallway. Could no smile or nod and only

4

a "good morning" mean that the person is not sincere in his or her return greeting? Or could the person simply be in a hurry or thinking of something else?

- **Missed nonverbal cues.** Because nonverbal cues are often subtle and delivered quickly, it is possible to miss or overlook them entirely. Should this occur, you will receive only part of the person's message and could potentially misinterpret the meaning.

- **Overemphasis of certain cues.** Traditionally, people place more importance on some nonverbal cues than on others. As a result, you may be tempted to overlook some signals and attribute more meaning to others. For example, in an interview, you may interpret an applicant's crossed arms, sitting back in the chair, and lack of smiling as arrogant indifference. Could the applicant simply be physically cold, insecure, or ill?

- **Cultural differences.** Each cultural and social group assigns meaning to nonverbal signals based on the values of that group. Trying to interpret cues sent by members of groups outside your own while applying your group's standards can lead to serious problems. You may end up with a total breakdown in communication.

- **Inconsistency of messages.** People use the same cues at different times to send various messages. This can lead to frustration if you are trying to interpret meaning. For example, a person backing away from you as you speak to him or her may mean that he or she is late for a meeting, bored with you, or has sun coming through the window into his or her eyes, or that you simply have bad breath.

Nonverbal Cue Interpretation

To get an idea of how well you interpret nonverbal meanings of others, solicit cooperation from several friends, co-workers, or family members over the next few days. Explain that your goal is to better interpret nonverbal cues. As you observe these people, do the following:

1. **Identify the behavior as you observe it.** For example, "I've noticed that you seem to be fidgeting with your pencil and looking at your watch as we talk."

2. **Ask for meaning clarification.** For example, "Would you please tell me what you are thinking about and what those signals mean?"

3. **Give feedback about your interpretation of their cues.** This allows them the chance to improve their own nonverbal communication behavior. They may not even be aware that they play with pencils or fidget when conversing. For example, "What I interpreted your signals to mean was that you were pressed for time and anxious to end the conversation."

4

IMPACT OF NONVERBAL CUES

In the United States, specific emotions and values traditionally are associated with nonverbal cues. You may have been taught these values or emotions in childhood and not realized you were learning them. See whether any of these are familiar to you (keep in mind that culture plays a big role in these instances).

Nonverbal Cue	Potential Emotion/Value
Pointing your finger at someone.	Rudeness; makes people uneasy/defensive.
Staring.	Rudeness; might make people uncomfortable, self-conscious, or angry.
Speaking softly in libraries, hospitals, and churches.	Respect for others.
Ladies sitting with their knees together.	Politeness; shows high moral values.
Looking at people as you talk to them.	Courtesy; allows reading of nonverbal cues.
Smiling.	Warmth, trustworthiness, and approachability.
Showing off (excessive jewelry, flashy items)	Alienation of others; makes others self-conscious; indicates arrogance.
Picking your nose.	Offensive; distracting; poor manners.

4

Nonverbal Cue Validation

1. Make two to three copies of the following list of nonverbal cues.

Nonverbal Cue	Interpretation
Smiling	
Crossed arms	
Crossed legs	
Frowning	
Nodding of head	
Pointing finger	
Hands on hips	
Playing with pencil	
Turning away slightly	
Looking away	
Lightly touching your knee	
Moving to within 18 to 24 inches	
Silence (in response to your question/comment)	

2. Work through the list of cues and describe how you would interpret each of them if you were talking to a co-worker of the same sex, race, and approximate age.

3. Give a blank copy of the list to several co-workers or friends.

4. Have your colleagues review the list and respond as if they were talking to someone of your sex, race, and approximate age.

5. Compare responses to help raise awareness of how people interpret the criteria differently based on their own age, sex, race, and value system.

6. Were the responses the same or different from each person completing the form? Explain.

7. What factors do you believe contributed to any differences noted?

_____

CULTURAL IMPACT ON NONVERBAL CUES

If you are not currently dealing with people of various racial, cultural, and socioeconomic backgrounds, you will likely be doing so soon because of projected changes in workplace demographics. To be successful in your interactions with people whose values and cultures differ from your own, you will need to broaden your scope of understanding of nonverbal signals. Examine the following situations and respond to each. Once you have completed all of them, turn to page 44 for possible answers.

4

■ Cultural Encounters

1. Your boss called this morning to say that a delegation of high-ranking Japanese diplomats and businesspeople will be touring your department in one hour. As they arrive, how should you greet them? Explain.

_____

_____

2. Your company uses foreign exchange students from the state university each summer. This year, a Malaysian student has been assigned to your department. It is the student's first trip away from home. On the second day on the job, the student passes by your open office door. You call him by name and use the traditional raised hand with index finger curled back and forth to beckon him to come into your office. Once in your office, you express your pleasure in having him on board and offer any assistance he may need. On the following morning, you hear from your assistant that the student confided in a co-worker that he thought you were arrogant and rude. What happened?

_____

_____

3. Recently, in a conversation with a young Iranian employee, you explained several job procedures and solicited her understanding of each process. In each instance, she smiled but shook her head back and forth (left to right). A bit flustered, you reexplained several times but continued to get the same response. Because you did not have time to continue, you rescheduled several hours the next day to go over the procedures again. Have you taken the appropriate action? Explain.

_____

_____

■ Possible Solutions[1]

1. Greet the delegates with a smile, nodding of the head, light handshake (firmness is a sign of aggressiveness in many countries), and avoid prolonged eye contact (staring is disrespectful to someone of high rank and is intimidating).

2. In many countries, the curled index finger is used only for calling animals and is considered an impolite gesture. You possibly offended the student.

3. Training is probably not necessary, since she was indicating understanding. In Iran and many other countries, shaking the head back and forth is the same as shaking the head up and down in the United States—an affirmative response.

TYPICAL NONVERBAL CUES

Entire books and years of research have been dedicated to the study of nonverbal cues and their meaning. To be more effective in your interpersonal relationships, you should continue to explore the topic to

_____

[1] Source: Derived from information in R E Axtell, *Gestures: The Do's and Taboos of Body Language around the World* (New York: John Wiley & Sons, 1991).

better learn how to "read" others' signals. Keep in mind that culture, values, and a variety of other factors contribute to meaning. Because of the possibility of easy misinterpretation, do not assume meaning based solely on nonverbal cues. Here are some typical nonverbal cues along with potential meanings.

- **Posture.** By standing or sitting upright, or leaning toward or away from someone, you send many different messages.

- **Eye contact.** By focusing on the facial area (eyes, nose, forehead), you can send a variety of messages. Depending on the duration of your stare, you can demonstrate interest, disinterest, physical attraction, contempt, or a variety of other emotions.

- **Nodding.** Shaking your head up and down generally means agreement, acknowledgment, or approval.

- **Crossing arms across the chest.** Typically viewed as a closed or defiant gesture, it could signal that you are cold or simply do not know where else to put your hands.

- **Smiling.** Generally viewed as a warm, friendly gesture, although it could be a mask of your uneasiness or embarrassment.

- **Pointing the index finger, pen/pencil, or other object.** You can use this gesture to make a strong point, but generally it is considered rude and challenging. Use these gestures with caution.

- **Hands on hips.** Almost always viewed as defiant, authoritarian, or a closed gesture, although you could be simply resting your hands.

- **Hand gestures.** Movements and symbols using your hands can send a multitude of messages, both positive and negative. Keep in mind the cultural variances discussed earlier.

- **Touch.** You can send many types of messages with touch. Interpretations of your meaning will vary among people in different

4

circumstances. Because of the potential legal repercussions, it is a good idea to keep your hands to yourself in the workplace.

Spatial Cues

Most people have distances (proxemics) at which they are comfortable interacting with others. When these distances are not respected or are intruded upon, feelings of violation or defensiveness may result. Studies have shown that these are the approximate comfort zones in the United States:

- **Intimate distance (0 to 18 inches).** Typically reserved for your family and intimate relations.
- **Personal distance (18 inches to 4 feet).** Often reserved for your close friends and business colleagues.
- **Social/work distance (4 to 12 feet).** Usually maintained at casual business events and during business transactions.
- **Public distance (12 or more feet).** Probably maintained at large gatherings, activities, or presentations.

Voice Cues

In addition to the voice qualities (pitch, volume, rate, and articulation) discussed in Chapter 3, you can send nonverbal messages in other ways during verbal communication.

- **Pauses.** Use these to effectively punctuate a sentence, to allow time for reflection on what you said, or to indicate that you are waiting for a response.
- **Silence.** If you want to indicate that you are thinking about what has been said or to show defiance or indifference, use silence.
- **Word selection (semantics).** Your word choice can signal intelligence, arrogance, concern, and many other messages. Choose your words wisely.

Appearance/Grooming Cues

- **Clothing/accessories.** The appropriate choice of hairstyle, glasses, jewelry, fragrance, and accessories can make or break your image in the eyes of others. Give some thought to the message you want to send and then cultivate that image.

- **Hygiene.** One of the easiest ways to cause people to avoid you is to neglect your personal hygiene. Unkempt hair and clothing, dirty facial hair on men, dirt under fingernails, food between teeth, body odor, or other similar factors over which you have control but neglect can turn people away.

Additional Cues

- **Personal surroundings/habits.** The organization and contents of your office, cleanliness of your car, eating habits, and anything else you have control over can send powerful messages about your initiative, professionalism, and enthusiasm. Be conscious of the nonwork-related messages you send.

- **Time.** The amount of time you allot to job applicants, employees, and peers for meetings or interactions can send definite messages of their value to you.

- **Follow-through.** Whether or not you take promised action, the amount of effort you dedicate to the follow-through and the time between promised action and follow-through are all important in communicating your perceived feeling of the importance of others to you.

4

■ Expanding on What You Have Learned

1. Many factors are obvious when you observe the nonverbal cues of a productive, effective employee. When interviewing a job applicant, what kind of nonverbal factors might indicate whether the applicant will become a good employee?

   _____

   _____

2. Based on your workplace experiences, what nonverbal signals should you use when trying to sell an idea, product, or service to someone else? Which ones should you avoid?

   _____

   _____

3. Think about the best communicator you know in your workplace. What positive nonverbal cues does he or she use? What negative cues?

   _____

   _____

Chapter 4 Checkpoints

This chapter has dealt with ways to better communicate and to supplement your verbal messages. Here are some key points to remember:

✓ Most of your message meaning is delivered nonverbally.

✓ Do not read too much meaning into nonverbal signals. Culture, values, and a variety of other factors determine the sender's meaning.

✓ Throughout your life, you have learned the value of certain nonverbal cues. Use these to your advantage.

✓ Other people send out many nonverbal cues. Research, observe, and learn how to interpret these signals in an effort to better understand and interact with others.

5 | Better Relationships through Listening

This chapter will help you to:

- Realize the importance of effective listening in interpersonal relationships.
- Recognize barriers to effective listening.
- Determine characteristics of effective listeners.
- Identify listening styles and how they affect comprehension of and response to messages.
- Develop strategies for listening improvement.

Toby Timmons, a 53-year-old sales manager, is feeling extremely frustrated as he explains to his newest salesperson, Teresa Lyons, a variety of techniques for effectively making cold calls to customers. Teresa has been with Hardwell Industries for a little over eight months but has not been very successful in developing new client relationships. She joined the organization shortly after graduating near the top of her class from a well-known business college. Her degree was in sales management.

As usual, while Toby speaks to Teresa, he suspects that she is not focused on what he is saying. She occasionally looks away from Toby, glances at her watch, and often asks him to repeat statements. Frequently, as they talk, Teresa makes comments such as "That's not what my instructor taught in college" or "It seems that sending a direct mail solicitation before calling on new customers is a better approach for making new contacts."

Toby is at his wits' end and wonders what he is doing wrong and why he cannot get his ideas across to Teresa. ■

■ Questions to Consider

1. Who do you believe is having communication difficulties in this scenario? Explain.

   _____

   _____

2. What are barriers that might be inhibiting Teresa's ability to get Toby's message?

   _____

   _____

3. If you were Toby, what would you do to remedy the communication? Explain.

   _____

   _____

LISTENING SELF-CRITIQUE

To get a quick snapshot of how well you perceive your own listening effectiveness, answer these questions and then score yourself. Answer based on how you actually behave, not on how you think you should behave. Place a check mark in the appropriate column. Before beginning, make copies of the survey, distribute them to co-workers, and ask them to rate you. This will give you feedback on how others perceive your listening skills.

	Always	Sometimes	Never
1. When someone speaks to me, I stop what I am doing to focus on what the person is saying.	_____	_____	_____
2. I listen to people even if I disagree with what they are saying.	_____	_____	_____
3. When I am unsure of someone's meaning, I ask for clarification.	_____	_____	_____
4. I avoid daydreaming when listening to others.	_____	_____	_____
5. I focus on main ideas, not details, when someone speaks to me.	_____	_____	_____
6. While listening, I am also conscious of non-verbal cues sent by the speaker.	_____	_____	_____
7. I consciously block out noise when some-one speaks to me.	_____	_____	_____
8. I paraphrase the messages I receive to ensure that I understood the speaker's meaning.	_____	_____	_____
9. I wait until I have received a person's entire message before forming my response.	_____	_____	_____
10. When receiving constructive criticism, I lis-ten with an open mind.	_____	_____	_____

Rating key: Always = 5   **Sometimes** = 3   **Never** = 0
Add your total score. If you rated

40–50   Your listening is excellent.
30–39   Your listening is very good.
20–29   Your listening is good.
15–19   Your listening is fair.
10–14   Your listening is poor.

With this insight about your listening skills, focus on the methods outlined in this chapter for increasing your listening effectiveness.

THE IMPORTANCE OF LISTENING

As a supervisor, poor listening corresponds with personal and organizational failure and the breakdown of effective interpersonal relationships. You may have a listening problem if people you know regularly say things such as:

"Did you hear what I said?"

"Are you listening?"

"Will you pay attention to what I'm saying?"

"Do you have any questions?"

If you suspect that you have a listening problem, do not feel too bad. Research conducted by Dr. Ralph Nichols, and supported by others,[1] showed that the average white-collar worker demonstrates only a 25 percent listening efficiency rate. With this level of competency, it is no wonder that many people miss much of what is said to them.

Think about what such poor listening habits could mean in your own workplace. For example, if you had 10 employees and they each made a daily $10 mistake due to poor listening, by the end of the year (5 days $\times$ 52 weeks), they would have cost your organization $26,000 in losses. In addition to the tangible losses, employee frustration levels rise, morale drops, and absenteeism and turnover increase as a result of prolonged ineffective listening.

BARRIERS TO EFFECTIVE LISTENING

Many things can get in the way of effectively receiving and decoding messages from others in the workplace. These barriers were identified in Chapter 2 and can ultimately lead to damaged relationships and losses.

---

[1]Dr. Ralph C. Nichols, "Listening Is a 10-Part Skill," *Nation's Business* 45 (1957), p. 56.

As a supervisor, one major barrier you should be aware of is the use of emotionally provocative language. Certain words or phrases evoke anger, frustration, and resentment and should be avoided. Review the following list and create a less provocative alternative.

Potentially Provoking	Alternative
You must/have got to	_____
You should	_____
Because I said so.	_____
That's a silly/stupid thing to say.	_____
Your problem is	_____
You're always	_____
You never	_____
What you fail to understand is	_____
You do this all the time.	_____
I don't understand your problem.	_____
This is so simple.	_____

5

IDENTIFYING EFFECTIVE LISTENING CHARACTERISTICS

The following activities are designed to help you eliminate barriers and understand the significance of good listening, along with the characteristics involved in effective listening. After reading the questions or instructions, fill in th blanks.

List five people whom you have known during your lifetime and to whom you have gone to share information, discuss key issues, and/or ask advice. (List only their names and relationships for now.)

Name	Relationship	Rating
1. _____	_____	_____
2. _____	_____	_____
3. _____	_____	_____
4. _____	_____	_____
5. _____	_____	_____

Now that you have identified five people, think about how you would rate their listening ability: outstanding, excellent, above average, average, below average, or poor. Place the rating for each in the space provided next to their relationship above.

Regarding their manner of listening, what four words or characteristics would you use to describe each of the five people you have identified?

1. _____	_____	_____	_____
2. _____	_____	_____	_____
3. _____	_____	_____	_____
4. _____	_____	_____	_____
5. _____	_____	_____	_____

How would you rate your own listening ability? (Circle one.)

Outstanding   Excellent   Above Average

Average   Below Average   Poor

List four words or characteristics you would use to describe your own approach to listening in the workplace.

_____   _____   _____   _____

Are there any similarities between your characteristics and those of the listeners you identified as above average? If so, what are they?

If you do not see similarities, develop an action plan for improving your listening approach and focus on the characteristics you identified as being effective in your "above average" listeners.

Note: One way to check the accuracy of your perception of your own listening effectiveness is to ask several people in your workplace who know you well. Have them rate your listening effectiveness on the scale from outstanding to poor. Once they rate you, have them provide hints on how to improve your effectiveness. These submissions or ratings could be done anonymously to get more candid feedback. Once you get the information, analyze it and incorporate it into your action plan, as necessary.

CHARACTERISTICS OF EFFECTIVE AND INEFFECTIVE LISTENERS

In 1948 Ralph Nichols, the "father of listening," identified the attributes of effective and ineffective listeners as shown below.[2]

Effective Listeners	Ineffective Listeners
• Alert	• Apathetic
• Interested	• Inattentive
• Responsive	• Defensive
• Attending	• Disinterested
• Nondistracted	• Distracted

(continued)

[2] Ralph C. Nichols, "Factors Accounting for Differences in Comprehension of Materials Presented Orally in the Classroom," Doctoral dissertation, State University of Iowa, Iowa City, 1948. Cited in L.K. Steil, L.L. Barker, and K.W. Watson, "Effective Listening: Key to Your Success" (New York: McGraw-Hill, 1983), p. 56.

Effective Listeners	Ineffective Listeners
▪ Understanding	▪ Impatient
▪ Caring	▪ Emotional
▪ Cautious	▪ Self-centered
▪ Noninterrupting	▪ Quick to judge
▪ Empathetic	▪ Uncaring
▪ Patient	▪ Insensitive
▪ Other centered	
▪ Nonemotional	
▪ Effective evaluator	

IDENTIFYING YOUR LISTENING STYLES

If you think about various listening situations you have had, you probably will realize that you listen differently under varying circumstances. Just as with any of your other skills, you place varying degrees of effort based on your level of initiative, desire, or interest. A determining factor in these levels is the *reason* you are listening. For example, you probably listen differently in a social situation than you do in a business setting.

According to the Wolvin-Coakley Listening Taxonomy, the reasons for listening can be categorized into five distinct levels.[3] Each level can enhance or detract from your personal interaction at the time. Each level also depends on how you listen, the situation, and the other person's perception of your listening style. The five levels are as follows:

1. Discriminative listening. This is at the base of all your listening. At this level, you try to determine the significance of the auditory and

---

[3] These levels were first identified by A. D. Wolvin and C. G. Coakley in *Listening* (Dubuque, IA: Wm C Brown, 1992), pp. 164–166.

visual messages you receive to determine necessary actions to take. *Example*: You are in a staff meeting but are expecting an important phone call. Even though you are involved in conversation, you subconsciously screen out other noises to listen for a ringing phone.

2. Comprehensive listening. At this level of listening, you strive to understand the message or information you receive so that you may remember and recall it for later use. *Example*: You are introduced to a new peer or member of senior management and try to remember her name and as many details about her as possible. This allows personal recognition when you meet her or need to refer to her in the future.

3. Therapeutic listening. This is most often associated with helping others. *Example*: One of your employees comes to you with a problem and asks advice. You listen carefully and then determine the appropriate response or course of action to take.

5

4. Critical listening. This occurs when you try to evaluate the value of the message you have received. You first use discriminative listening to determine the significance of the message and then use comprehensive listening to understand. Then you analyze or assess the message and make a judgment. *Example*: You listen to a salesperson explain a product or service to determine whether you need it or not.

5. Appreciative listening. This involves discriminative and comprehensive listening; however, your primary purpose is to derive pleasure or satisfaction from messages you receive. *Example*: A co-worker comes to you and relates a funny incident or joke.

Expanding on What You Have Learned

Keeping in mind the concepts outlined in this chapter, answer the following questions.

1. In your current work environment, what can you do to increase overall listening effectiveness?

   _____

   _____

2. Looking at the barriers identified earlier, what type of leader would you associate with those types of situations and what image do you have of that kind of person?

_____

_____

3. What steps or actions do you plan to take to increase your listening effectiveness?

_____

_____

4. In your workplace, which of the five identified styles of listening do you use most often? How can you use other styles on a more frequent basis in order to increase your effectiveness and strengthen relationships?

_____

_____

Chapter 5 Checkpoints

As you work to develop better listening skills and improve relationships, keep the following points in mind:

✓ Pay attention to how others respond to your listening patterns.

✓ Strive to eliminate language that causes listening barriers.

✓ Identify positive listening characteristics in others and use them yourself.

✓ Define your purpose for listening in each situation; then listen appropriately.

6 | Personal Management Style and Relationships

"We need to take a serious look at the way we're dealing with employee needs, Boss," declared Josh Randall, a supervisor in a branch office of TriState Federal Savings and Loan. He continued, "We can't keep using the same systems of rewarding, coaching, counseling, and managing people we've always used and expect that they will work."

Josh's boss, Connie Marshal, has heard this speech before but has held firm in her stance that things were fine at TriState.

Josh went on to restate his belief that just because deposits seemed stable and employee turnover had not significantly increased, the potential for disaster loomed. He reminded Connie that other financial institutions were going through some pretty bad times. And, while he had to admit those problems might not have been performance related, the ultimate outcomes had affected the opinions and increased the concerns of TriState employees.

Josh added, "Have you noticed the change in our workforce in the past five years?" He continued without waiting for a response, "We've got more older employees being trained, and in the past year alone, we've hired eight members of minority groups and two employees with disabilities."

Connie conceded that things had changed in regard to the workforce makeup but stated, "I really don't see why you feel these changes justify a change in our approach to management." As Josh rose to leave, he countered, "Fine, but don't say I didn't warn you." ■

6

▮ Questions to Consider

1. Could the changes alluded to by Josh have an impact at TriState? Explain.

_____

_____

2. What do you think of Josh's approach in discussing the topic with Connie? Could it have been improved? Explain.

_____

_____

3. Why do you think Connie might be so complacent about Josh's suggestions? Explain.

_____

_____

4. Assuming that Josh is correct, what are some possible results of Connie's reluctance to change the way their organization deals with employee needs? Why?

_____

_____

THREE TRADITIONAL STYLES OF MANAGEMENT

You might choose from a variety of management styles to manage your employees. Three styles have been identified, each with its own set of advantages and disadvantages and with distinct effects on supervisor-employee relationships. Select your style based on your desired outcomes and the personalities of the people with whom you are involved. Because human nature is so complex and no two situations are identical, you can be most effective by matching your management style to the current situation. The three traditional styles are as follows:

- **Autocratic.** You maintain tight control and you or your supervisor make virtually all decisions.
- **Democratic.** You encourage employees to provide ideas and advice or to recommend possible solutions before decisions are made.
- **Free rein.** You give employees virtual autonomy for goal setting, for behavior, and for decision making. You play a minimal role and act basically as an adviser or coach.

The following table identifies the major advantages and disadvantages of each style.

6

Style	Advantages	Disadvantages
Autocratic	• Expedites decision making • Requires only one person for decision making • Reduces meeting requirements • Good in emergencies	• Doesn't develop employee decision-making skills • Can prohibit productivity, creativity, and initiative. • Can negatively affect morale • Can increase tardiness and absenteeism • Tends to alienate people over extended periods of time
Democratic	• Can ultimately increase productivity and quality • Facilitates employee involvement • Can increase morale • Can decrease tardiness, absenteeism, and turnover • Builds employee support • Helps develop mutual trust • Fosters partnerships	• Increases time needed for decision making • Bogs down the system due to increased involvement • Can initially slow productivity • Takes skill to manage
Free rein	• Employees develop their own goals and leadership skills • Employee morale may increase due to virtually complete autonomy • Relaxed approach to task completion • Works well in team environments with professionals who need little guidance	• Lack direct supervisory guidance • Hard to distinguish supervisors from employees • No one person has accountability • Significantly reduces supervisory effectiveness • Can be difficult to monitor individual performance • May result in a relaxed approach to task completion

THE IMPACT OF MANAGEMENT STYLES

Quality of work life (QWL) is a term often used to describe the satisfaction and self-fulfillment experienced by employees at various organizational levels. QWL is derived from opportunities given by management that allow employees to have input into decision making and to influence their own work environment. This may seem like a relatively simple concept, but it requires a major effort on the part of many supervisors and managers. The reason for the difficulty is that QWL can occur only when there is a willingness to give up control or adopt a more relaxed style of management. A top-down or hierarchical management style will only inhibit or block employee productivity, creativity, and the willingness to pitch in to do more than the job requires. In effect, a strict style of management not only impedes progress and results but also can harm the supervisor-employee relationship.

Excuses for Retaining Power

Too often you might be reluctant to give up or share your power with employees. Some reasons supervisors typically give for a similar reluctance include the following:

- They feel that they have earned their authority and don't want to give it away.
- They feel they are supposed to control.
- They don't know how to delegate or empower others.
- They feel they may be viewed as weak or ineffective.
- Their supervisors manage them the same way they manage others (learned behavior).

Can you think of other excuses?

■ Personal Reflection

Think about a time when you knew a very autocratic or controlling supervisor or manager.

1. What type of interpersonal relationships existed between that person and his or her employees?

_____

_____

6

2. Were there opportunities missed by the supervisor, his or her employee(s), or the organization due to limited interpersonal interactions? Explain.

_____

_____

3. What would have made the relationships more productive and successful?

_____

_____

As you determine which management style is best for you, think about the possible repercussions of failing to establish sound relationships and trust with your employees. Too often, inadequate consideration and time are spent developing and nurturing the supervisor-employee relationship. To help prevent potential breakdowns with your employees, you may want to follow these suggestions:

- **Develop positive relationships immediately.** With new employees, your relationship starts during the employment interview. That is when the employees' initial impression of you is formed. Once hired, they begin to solidify their opinions based on your communication and interpersonal style. (Specific techniques for accomplishing this foundation building is provided in another book in this series, _Coaching Skills: A Guide for Supervisors._)

- **Set performance goals.** Working with your employees, set specific, attainable, and measurable goals for them to work toward. Nothing is more frustrating for you or your employees than getting to performance appraisal time and wondering how the employees have performed.

- **Continually provide support.** Most people need and seek an environment that nurtures and offers opportunities for growth.

- **Give ongoing feedback.** As you saw in Chapter 2, feedback is a vital factor in the interpersonal communication process. Through feedback you let employees know how you perceive their performance and they let you know their thoughts.

- **Encourage open communication.** Your efforts in declaring and demonstrating that you desire and welcome effective two-way communication will lead to your success and your employees' success.

- **Develop an understanding of individuals.** Humans are a complex species. The more you read and learn about behavior, the stronger you will become as a leader. Focus your attention on the strengths of your employees, rather than their differences.

- **Personalize your management style.** To strengthen your supervisory effectiveness, you will need to relate to each employee in a manner that takes into account their individual abilities and personality. Drawing from the spectrum of styles discussed earlier, you should match your approach to each employee and situation for maximum effectiveness.

6

- **Take time to be concerned about your people.** Show employees that you are concerned for their emotional, personal, and professional well-being. If employees are having personal problems, assist them in getting the resources needed to solve them. If they are experiencing on-the-job difficulty, investigate and provide appropriate guidance and support.

- **Show an interest in your employees' off-the-job lives.** This does not mean imposing on their privacy if they do not want to share information. What it does mean is that if you make the effort to get to know your employees as people, you can often strengthen bonds of trust and increase on-the-job cooperation.

- **Establish firm two-way communication.** Your employees should feel that they can come to you at any time to ask a question, to seek guidance, or to make a suggestion. One way to determine how strong your relationships are would be to think of each employee and ask yourself, "When did this person last drop into my office just to chat?"

6

- **Involve employees in decisions that affect them.** This satisfies an innate desire for control that many people seem to have. It also encourages employees to think and participate. When employees help make decisions, they are less likely to criticize the outcomes.

- **Manage for success.** Not many people set out to fail when they work on a project. If they do fail, they often look for reasons to point a finger at someone else or to cast blame. To ensure that you are not the recipient of such accusations, always work toward providing win-win situations. In such an environment, when the employee succeeds, so do you and the organization.

- **Take calculated risks.** Nobody likes a fool, so ensure that your ventures are well planned and executed. If you involve employees, make sure that you provide adequate support and guidance so their success is more likely.

- **Avoid game playing.** Be open, honest, and sincere with your employees. Your success often depends on the relationships you build with them. If you damage those relationships, you may regret it in the future.

- **Use creative problem-solving techniques.** Avoid using the same tired approaches for every situation. Analyze and address each situation with an open mind and involve your employees. This may lead to more efficient and productive solutions.

FACTORS AFFECTING MANAGEMENT STYLE

Numerous factors influence your choice of management style(s). These include the following:

- **Education/training.** Exposure to a variety of management ideas and concepts in a learning environment often serves as a basis for on-the-job practical application later.

- **Your boss' management style(s).** You may treat your employees in a manner prescribed or demonstrated by your boss. For example, if your boss tends to be a very controlling, autocratic manager who demands strict compliance and rigid formality, you are likely to follow suit. While such mirroring may not be your preferred style, you may do it out of instinct to survive in your job.

- **Time constraints.** The amount of time available can influence your style. Democratic and free rein styles take longer than autocratic style because of the number of people involved in the decision-making process.

- **Policies and procedures.** As a supervisor, your employees and your manager expect you to know, interpret, and enforce established policies and procedures. These guidelines often dictate your actions and the parameters within which you do your job.

- **Personal beliefs and values.** Your own perspectives about people, your job, the organization, and your own roles will impact the manner in which you supervise others.

- **Your self-esteem.** If you have confidence in your own abilities and self-worth, you will likely be more flexible and receptive to involvement and new ideas from your employees and others.

- **Organizational culture.** The nature and structure of your organization, along with the general atmosphere within the environment, can affect your approach to management.

Expanding on What You Have Learned

The fact that there is no "one answer" or "right way" to manage people can be frustrating. The key is to remain flexible and communicate in any encounter with your employees. With that in mind, respond to the following questions.

1. What are some ways to identify the best technique(s) for managing a specific employee?

   _____

   _____

2. How can you use a variety of management styles and improve your overall effectiveness in your workplace?

   _____

   _____

3. Why do you think many supervisors find it difficult to effectively manage certain members of their departments?

   _____

   _____

6

Chapter 6 Checkpoints

Managing a cross-section of personalities is an exciting challenge. As you interact with your staff, remember the following:

✓ Quality of work life (QWL) can be improved by a willingness to involve employees.

✓ There is no one "best" style to manage people.

✓ Many factors influence the ways you manage others.

✓ To improve your management style, you must be willing to allow employees to grow.

✓ By understanding human nature, you gain insights into how to effectively manage.

✓ Your most significant gains in working with others will come from your flexibility.

7 | Conflict in Interpersonal Relationships

This chapter will help you to:

- Identify the types of conflict that might affect you and your employees.
- Recognize sources of conflict.
- Develop strategies for dealing with conflict.
- See the impact of low commitment levels on goal attainment.
- Salvage relationships following conflict.

During another typical Monday morning staff meeting, the members of the Training & Development Department could not agree on how to best service their customers. The department has many opportunities to add value to the organization, but prioritizing always has been a challenge.

The director, Tom Lawrence, and Renee Diamond, a senior training specialist, disagree over the use of outside training consultants. Renee argued, "Tom, I think it is ridiculous for us to continue to spend thousands of dollars per quarter on outsiders who know virtually nothing about our company. Many of them simply take a preexisting program, put our company name on the front and in the case studies, call it customized, and then charge a hefty fee."

Tom countered, "Renee, I know how you feel; we've been through this dozens of times before. If it were up to you, we'd hire a couple of new trainers, pay them salary and benefits, and do all of our own training design."

Renee jumped in, "You're right, Tom. I believe we would be better off from a quality control and service standpoint having our own people available all the time. They could design, present, and consult internally, as needed."

Tom was getting frustrated and stated, "Listen, Renee. I appreciate your concerns and value your opinion, but we'll continue to use outside consultants as needed." He added, "And that's just the way it is—end of discussion."

Feeling defeated and angered, Renee reluctantly sat back, crossed her arms, and sighed. ■

7

■ Questions to Consider

1. What seem to be some of the visible and subtle issues in this scenario?

   _____

   _____

2. How do you think Tom handled the conflict? Explain.

   _____

   _____

3. Can you think of anything that Renee might have done differently to change the outcome of this encounter? Explain.

   _____

   _____

WHAT IS CONFLICT?

Conflict often results when two or more people, departments, or organizations disagree. It should be viewed as neither positive nor negative. Instead, conflict is an opportunity to help meet organizational goals and often leads to healthy competition.

It is not unusual for you to encounter some sort of conflict during your daily workplace routine. In fact, conflict is normal and beneficial as long as it remains issue oriented, rather than personality oriented. If you keep conflict focused on an issue without attacking the people involved, you can use conflict to effectively uncover and resolve a variety of needs.

TYPES OF CONFLICT

Whenever you have individuals interacting, you have the potential for conflict. There are five potential forms of conflict in organizations.

7

Form	Example
1. Between individuals	Two employees disagree on the correct procedure for completing an assignment.
2. Between an individual and a group	One team member opposes the decision of the rest of the team.
3. Between organizational groups	One department has a goal that places additional operational requirements or workloads on another department.
4. Between organizations	Two organizations are marketing similar products or services to the same customer group.
5. Between an individual and an organization	A dissatisfied customer feels that a company is not providing quality products or services.

SOURCES OF CONFLICT

Potentially, any issue can lead to conflict. For that reason, you need to understand why conflict occurs to manage it effectively. Here are some common causes of conflict.

- **Differing values and beliefs.** These sometimes create situations in which the perception of an issue or its impact varies. Because values and beliefs have been learned over long periods of time and are often taken personally at face value, individuals get very defensive when their "foundations" are challenged. *Example*: A person has been taught that it is ethically and morally wrong to lie to a customer, yet you tell him it is okay to tell "a little white lie" to explain a missed delivery.

- **Varying perceptions.** People often witness or view an incident or issue differently. This can cause disagreement, frustration, and many other emotional feelings. *Example*: One employee tells you that he is upset because he missed a deadline because another employee did not effectively manage her time. The accused employee reminds you that you had taken her off the project in question to work on another assignment. This resulted in missing the original assignment deadline and led to a perception that she could not manage time.

- **Inadequate or poor communication.** Any time there is inadequate communication, the chance for conflict escalates. *Example*: An angry employee comes to you because a less-tenured employee received a promotion that he felt should have been offered to him. You meant to tell the employee that a new department is being formed and that you have recommended him to manage it. This newly created position is actually a higher level than the one involved in the promotion.

- **Goals that do not match.** Frustration and resentment can result from misaligned efforts. *Example*: You have budgeted to allow an employee to attend a seminar that you believe would improve her current skills; however, she wants to take a college course to help qualify her for a promotion.

- **Opposition over shared resources.** When two people or groups vie for the same resources, conflict usually results. *Example*: All funds for equipment purchase in your organization are lumped into a central account. Both you and the supervisors from another department have a "priority" project requiring the purchase of equipment. There is only enough money for one purchase.

- **Personal style differences.** Each person is different and requires special consideration and a unique approach in interactions. *Example*: You have an employee who is quiet and calm, yet effective in her work. You also have a very vocal, boisterous, and self-confident employee. If you use a direct, critical approach to correct an error with both, you may get tears from the first employee and defensiveness from the second.

- **Outcomes dependent on others.** Whenever you have two or more people, departments, or organizations working jointly toward goal attainment, the potential for conflict exists. *Example*: Your company produces a piece of equipment that is sold to another organization for distribution to customers. The component parts for the equipment come from two other companies. If there is a breakdown at any point in the production or distribution system, the end customer could become dissatisfied due to delays or nonavailability of equipment.

- **Contrary expectations.** When one party expects something not provided by another, conflict will likely result. *Example*: Your company offers a 90-day "parts-only" warranty on equipment that you sell; however, when it breaks down within that period, the customer expects free service also. If it is not rendered, the customer might be dissatisfied.

- **Inconsistent management styles.** People generally like to know what to expect and do not want surprises from their supervisor. When they get mixed signals due to inconsistency, they could become frustrated and conflict could result. *Example*: You allow one employee opportunities or privileges not granted to other employees.

- **Misuse of power.** Resentment, frustration, and retaliation often result when employees believe that their supervisor is abusing authority or power. *Example*: You tell an attractive employee that unless certain sexual favors are granted, he will not receive a desired promotion.

■ Personal Reflection

One way to learn to deal with conflict effectively is to examine how you have handled it in the past. Take a few minutes to think of situations in the past month when you experienced some form of conflict with an individual, group, or organization. Explain what happened, why it occurred, how you felt about it, and different possible actions that you could have taken to resolve it.

_____

_____

_____

_____

IMPACT OF CONFLICT ON GOAL ATTAINMENT

Mutual support between you and your employees is crucial to the successful attainment of organizational goals. Unless all parties form a cohesive unit, productivity and possibilities of individual success are significantly reduced. Additionally, if you and your employees fail to support each other or contribute maximum effort toward achievement of established objectives, all of you could fail. For example, if all team members have a high degree of commitment and are working toward goal attainment, but you do not support their efforts because of some conflict, success levels will be reduced and productivity limited. Along the same lines, if your support level is high but your employees are not doing their part, your chance of success is reduced. Only when both are working together can goals be achieved. The figure on page 81 illustrates this concept.

Supervisory support

		High	Low
Team effort	High	Increased	Reduced
	Low	Reduced	Reduced

GUIDELINES FOR CONFLICT MANAGEMENT

Mismanaged conflict can create serious problems for you and your employees in the workplace. Even though situations and personalities will differ, some basic approaches may help you resolve your conflicts. Try these.

- **Be proactive in avoiding conflict.** As a supervisor, you must know the personalities of your employees, their capabilities, and the environments most conducive to their effectiveness. Use each person in ways that allow only win-win situations; do not set your employees up for conflict or failure.

- **Identify and confront underlying issues immediately.** Because of the emotional issues often involved, few people enjoy dealing with conflict. If you fail to acknowledge and confront issues as soon as they become known, however, tensions may escalate.

- **Clarify communication.** Ensure that you solicit information on the causes of the conflict and provide the clear, detailed feedback necessary to resolve the issue.

- **Remain calm.** You cannot be part of the solution if you become part of the problem. If you are one of the factors contributing to the conflict, consider getting an objective third party, possibly your supervisor, to arbitrate.

- **Stress cooperation rather than competition.** One of your roles is to ensure that all employees work together toward common goals. When one employee succeeds at the expense of another's failure, you have not done your job. Encourage and develop teamwork.

- **Focus resolution efforts on the issues.** Do not get caught up in or allow finger-pointing, name-calling, or accusations. Keep all efforts and discussions directed toward identifying and resolving the real issue(s).

- **Keep an open mind.** Avoid letting your own values or beliefs influence your objectivity when working toward conflict resolution.

- **Establish procedures for handling conflict.** It is easier to implement a process already in place than to have to come up with one quickly. That is why most customer service organizations have set customer complaint–handling procedures.

SALVAGING RELATIONSHIPS FOLLOWING CONFLICT

Managing conflict involves more than just resolving the disagreement. If you fail to address the emotional and psychological needs of those involved, you may find the conflict returning and/or severe damage to the relationship as a result.

Depending on the severity of the conflict and how it was handled at each stage, it may be impossible to go back to where you were before. The key to reducing such potential is to identify and address conflicting issues as early as possible. The longer a conflict exists, the more damage it can cause. Whenever possible, apply one of the following strategies to help protect and salvage the relationship(s) between yourself, your employees, and whoever else is involved.

1. **Reaffirm the value of the relationship.** You cannot assume that others feel the same way you do or understand your intent

unless you communicate it. Tell them how much you value your relationship.

2. **Demonstrate commitment.** You must verbalize and demonstrate your desire to continue or strengthen your relationship.

3. **Be realistic.** Because of personality styles, it is difficult for some people to "forgive and forget." You have to systematically help restore their trust.

4. **Remain flexible.** A solid relationship involves the ability to give and take. It is especially crucial for individuals to be able to make concessions following conflict.

5. **Keep communication open.** One of the most common causes of conflict and destroyed relationships is poor communication.

6. **Gain commitment.** You cannot do it all by yourself. Get a commitment to work toward reconciliation from any other people involved in the conflict.

7. **Monitor progress.** Do not assume that because the conflict was resolved it will remain that way. Deep-seated issues often resurface, especially when commitment was not obtained.

7

Expanding on What You Have Learned

Think about what you have read in this chapter as you respond to the following questions.

1. What are some of the policies and procedures in your organization that currently do, or potentially could, lead to conflict?

   _____

   _____

2. As a supervisor, how can you prevent conflict among your employees, peers, and customers?

   _____

   _____

3. Once conflict is resolved, how do you currently monitor it to ensure that it does not return?

_____

_____

4. In your organization, who do you go to when conflicts escalate, and what is the individual supposed to do about them? Does this system work? Can you think of a better alternative?

_____

_____

7

Chapter 7 Checkpoints

Conflict can be debilitating for employees and organizations. To help reduce or eliminate it in your organization, remember these key points:

✓ Conflict that is issue oriented *can* be positive and result in change.

✓ To deal effectively with conflict, you must recognize its sources:
- Differing values and beliefs.
- Varying perceptions.
- Inadequate or poor communication.
- Goals that do not match.
- Opposition over shared resources.
- Personal style differences.
- Outcomes dependent on others.
- Contrary expectations.
- Inconsistent management style.
- Misuse of power.

✓ The amount of support provided by a supervisor determines the level of employee and organizational success.

✓ Conflict resolution is facilitated by following standard guidelines.

✓ Once conflict is reduced, you must work toward reestablishing relationships.

8 | Change in the Workplace

This chapter will help you to:

- Realize the impact that change has on workplace relationships.
- Identify how a variety of diversity issues affect relationships.
- Redefine the way you supervise the changing workforce.
- Pinpoint changes occurring in your workplace.

Malcom Williams is having trouble understanding his employees. Carrie Olson, a 17-year-old Caucasian cashier, continually shows up late for work, regularly asks to leave early on Friday afternoons, yet tearfully begs Malcom to let her continue to work because she needs the job and salary. Lucille, a 58-year-old black employee, has never been late, volunteers to work overtime, and must be forced to take a vacation. Then there is a 32-year-old Iranian, Mohammed, who has been with the company only seven months. Mohammed constantly challenges Malcom's decisions, asking why things must be done. He also requests special training to qualify himself for a better job, goes to college three nights a week, and keeps insisting that he is ready for a promotion. ■

■ Questions to Consider

1. Do you believe that age, race, or sex has anything to do with the way Malcom's employees are acting? Explain.

   _____

   _____

2. Do you believe the issues Malcom is dealing with are normal for a supervisor? Explain.

_____

_____

3. What are some strategies that Malcom might use to deal with Carrie? Lucille? Mohammed?

_____

_____

THE CHANGING WORKPLACE

The workplace is changing rapidly and requires supervisors to continually upgrade their people skills and knowledge. Each year brings about new terminology and changes: Workforce 2000, diversity, paradigm shifts, globalization, glass ceilings, postbaby boomers, job sharing, telecommuticating, and the Americans with Disabilities Act, to name a few. Did you know that in the past decade,

- Nearly half of all U.S. companies were restructured?
- Over 80,000 firms were acquired or merged?
- Several hundred thousand companies were downsized?
- At least 700,000 organizations sought bankruptcy protection?
- Over 450,000 companies failed?[1]

No longer can a talented technician be successfully promoted into supervision without receiving additional training in basic people management skills. Supervising people in today's business world involves far more than just being a nice person who knows the company or job well. People,

---

[1] Price Pritchett and Ron Pound, *The Employee Handbook for Organizational Change* (Dallas, TX: Pritchett Publishing Company, 1993).

events, and the business world have become far too complex for that. The biggest challenge for today's supervisor is adapting to all these changes.

Change Assessment

Do a quick workplace attitude check. If you are like most people in the workplace, you probably have heard or made negative comments about changing situations. Put a check by familiar comments. Then think about the impact of each on you, your employees, and your organization.

_____	Why don't they just leave well enough alone?
_____	Why do we have to change _____? It's not going to make a difference.
_____	We tried _____ before and it didn't work. It won't work now either.
_____	Nothing changes but the changes!
_____	This (change) too shall pass.
_____	We'll just dig in and wait for this to pass.
_____	Every time I learn the game, they change the rules on me.
_____	I'm so busy making changes, I can't get my job done.
_____	Change is good, as long as I'm not involved.
_____	If it ain't broke, why are we fixing it?

8

CHANGES AFFECTING WORKPLACE RELATIONSHIPS

Entire books have been written on changing events that affect how supervisors and employees interact in the workplace. In addition to information here, you may want to do further research.

Some of the events affecting you, your employees, and your organization are as follows.

- **Reshaping of the work environment.** Through mergers, acquisitions, foreclosures, flattening, and a myriad of other events, it is estimated that millions of employees leave their jobs or change careers each year. The result is a keen need for employees and supervisors who have "transferable skills," such as effective interpersonal and communication skills.

- **Shifts from a production to a service environment.** For employees and organizations to successfully make this shift from primarily production-oriented environments, employees will need training to learn how to deal effectively with people. Good service is no longer nice to have; both internal customers (people within your organization) and external customers demand it. Your job is to identify and provide resources for employee learning.

- **Increases in diversity awareness.** Projections from the U.S. Department of Labor and numerous other sources point to a marked increase in the number of employees entering the workforce who are in a minority group, female, disabled, and/or over the age of 40. With these groups comes a need for supervisors to educate themselves and their employees about the values and beliefs of each group in order to draw from available group member strengths.

- **Formation of team-based work units.** Many companies already are successfully using the "team" approach in which the supervisors adopt a coaching or co-worker role rather than an autocratic one. To function in such an environment will require you to learn how to effectively use teams and to make a shift in your thinking. Failure to do so could lead to conflict and ultimately failure for you and your team.

- **Demographic shifts in the workforce.** In the past 20 years, there has been a shift in the age of Americans. The potential labor pool has aged as the "baby boomers" born in the 1950s grow older and start to "grey." Additionally, the "post–baby boomers" born in the mid-1960s are fewer in number. This reduced labor pool and shift in age groups could present scheduling and employment challenges for you in the future.

- **Shifts in values and work ethics.** A number of people believe that today many younger workers and those new to the workforce have an attitude of "what's in it for me?" Sometimes referred to as the "now" generation because of a desire for instant gratification or success, members of this group are often seen as being impatient and arrogant. As a group, they are also often better educated than previous workers. These younger employees may require you to be better informed, more patient, and to act as a facilitator or mentor rather than as a traditional order giver.

IMPACT OF CHANGES

With the wide spectrum of changes occurring in society, particularly in your workplace, your job as a supervisor continues to become increasingly more complicated. You are probably or will soon be dealing with groups of people and legal, cultural, and technological issues on a far more complex and regular basis than ever before. You will be forced to adapt your approach to accommodate new issues. The following are some of these issues:

- **Gender.** For years there have been instances and reports of inequality in pay, sexual harassment, and employment discrimination because of a person's sex. As a supervisor, you must be aware that this exists. You also must be aware of the laws that have been passed to reduce their likelihood. You must help raise your employees' awareness and sensitivity levels on gender issues.

- **Technology.** Advances in computers and automation are moving at an unbelievable pace. Their existence creates a phenomenal technological resource for you. For you to take full advantage of the capabilities of various technological advances and supervise employees using them, you will have to retool your own skills. By becoming more knowledgeable about technology, you can streamline tasks and staff functions. You also can allay fears of employees who might feel that their job is threatened by increased automation. By redefining their job descriptions, cross-training, retraining, and communicating with each employee, you can turn technology into a valuable asset.

- **Age.** Like gender issues, the change in the makeup of the workforce has increased the need to deal fairly with all age groups. It is vital to understand that as the population matures, the values, beliefs, and motivational needs gradually shift. As a supervisor, you are challenged to be all things to all groups by providing support, encouragement, and needs satisfaction to all your employees.

- **Disability.** Since the passage of the Americans with Disabilities Act of 1990, more supervisors are consciously striving to provide equal access to all employment-related opportunities for the disabled worker. You will need to be aware of accommodations that can be made to allow employees with disabilities to perform job tasks. You also will need to educate other employees about disabilities in an effort to relieve apprehension and increase interpersonal effectiveness for yourself and your employees.

- **Race/ethnicity.** This has been an ongoing issue for supervisors for decades and will intensify if future demographic projections are correct. For you to function and provide a supportive environment in which all employees can flourish, divisiveness fostered by ethnic and racial differences must be eliminated from your workplace. Although it is probably not totally possible, it is a goal toward which you can strive.

VALUING DIVERSITY

With such a wide cross-section of society represented in many organizations, you probably have an opportunity to interact with and tap into a resource pool that traditionally has been limited to certain areas of the country. By intentionally working toward stronger interpersonal relationships with your employees, you will be able to identify skills and knowledge that can be specifically focused on workplace initiatives.

Contributions of Diversity

Take a few minutes to think about the various work groups identified in this chapter. Identify and list as many work-related strengths offered by each group as possible. Also list possible applications in your organization. An example has been provided to get you started.

Group	Strengths	Possible Workplace Advantage
Over 40	*Experienced in workforce*	*Can be used to train others*
18-39		
Other-than-caucasian		
Female		
Male		
Disabled		

TIPS FOR SURVIVING CHANGE

As a supervisor, your job involves making recommendations and offering advice to your supervisor before changes are made. Once the decision to change is made, your job is to support it. Remember that your employees look to you as a role model. If you are reluctant to embrace the change, your employees will likely act in a similar fashion. To reduce frustrations and increase the likelihood of harmonious change, try to do the following:

- Set a positive example.
- Demonstrate your support for the change.
- Encourage employees to accept the change.
- Keep your employees and your boss informed about the change.
- Focus on the benefits of the change to keep your own morale up.

- Make necessary mental and skill adaptations to implement the change.
- Support your boss.

Expanding on What You Have Learned

Use the answers to these questions to help you adapt to changes in your workplace and strengthen your supervisor-employee relationships.

1. What changes do you expect in your organization within the coming year? (If unsure, discuss with your supervisor before answering.)

   _____

   _____

2. How will these changes affect you? Your employees?

   _____

   _____

3. Are you currently openly discussing changes that affect your workplace with your employees? How is that being done? Is there a better way to communicate the information?

   _____

   _____

4. Can you list at least three ways to better involve your employees in workplace change decisions? What potential benefit does each technique provide?

   _____

   _____

Chapter 8 Checkpoints

Adapting effectively to change is crucial to ensuring a healthy work environment and strong relationships between you and your employees. Keep these points in mind:

✓ The entire business world is experiencing ongoing change.

✓ To succeed in a changing environment, you will need to upgrade your people skills.

✓ Avoid negativity related to changing situations.

✓ Increasing your awareness of diversity issues makes it easier to relate to a wider number of workers.

✓ Team-based work units are a coming trend.

✓ Demographic shifts in society will present new challenges and will call for new skills.

✓ Values and work ethics are shifting and require patience and understanding.

Post-Test

Assess your knowledge related to building and maintaining effective interpersonal relationships by answering these questions.

1. From a trust-building standpoint, your key responsibility as a supervisor is to your _____.

2. There are three alternative approaches to building trust in your relationships. They are _____, _____, and _____.

3. True two-way communication can only occur when both parties are _____.

4. According to studies conducted by Albert Mehrabian, a larger portion of message meaning is derived from _____ and _____, rather than from the spoken word.

5. The easiest way to prevent misinterpretation of nonverbal cues is to _____.

6. There are basically five different listening levels. They are _____, _____, _____, _____, and _____.

7. Three traditional styles of management are _____, _____, and _____.

8. When selecting an approach to any management situation, you should consider _____ and the _____ with which you are dealing, and then use a _____.

POST-TEST ANSWERS

1. *people*

2. *defensive, supportive, collaborative*

3. *committed to the purpose of the interaction*

4. *vocal qualities and nonverbal cues*

5. *ask for clarification*

6. *discriminative, comprehensive, therapeutic, critical, appreciative*

7. *autocratic, democratic, free rein*

8. *desired outcomes, personalities, combination of strategies*

9. *disagreement between two or more people, departments, or organizations*

10. *people management skills*

9. Conflict results from a ——————————— .

10. The workplace is changing rapidly and requires supervisors to continually upgrade their ——————————— .

Business Skills Express Series

This growing series of books addresses a broad range of key business skills and topics to meet the needs of employees, human resource departments, and training consultants.

To obtain information about these and other Business Skills Express books, please call Irwin Professional Publishing toll free at 1-800-634-3966.

Effective Performance Management
ISBN 1-55623-867-3

Hiring the Best
ISBN 1-55623-865-7

Writing that Works
ISBN 1-55623-856-8

Customer Service Excellence
ISBN 1-55623-969-6

Writing for Business Results
ISBN 1-55623-854-1

Powerful Presentation Skills
ISBN 1-55623-870-3

Meetings that Work
ISBN 1-55623-866-5

Effective Teamwork
ISBN 1-55623-880-0

Time Management
ISBN 1-55623-888-6

Assertiveness Skills
ISBN 1-55623-857-6

Motivation at Work
ISBN 1-55623-868-1

Overcoming Anxiety at Work
ISBN 1-55623-869-X

Positive Politics at Work
ISBN 1-55623-879-7

Telephone Skills at Work
ISBN 1-55623-858-4

Managing Conflict at Work
ISBN 1-55623-890-8

The New Supervisor: Skills for Success
ISBN 1-55623-762-6

The *Americans with Disabilities Act:* What Supervisors Need to Know
ISBN 1-55623-889-4

Managing the Demands of Work and Home
ISBN 0-7863-0221-6

Effective Listening Skills
ISBN 0-7863-0102-4

Goal Management at Work
ISBN 0-7863-0225-9

Positive Attitudes at Work
ISBN 0-7863-0100-8

Supervising the Difficult Employee
ISBN 0-7863-0219-4

Cultural Diversity in the Workplace
ISBN 0-7863-0125-2

Managing Change in the Workplace
ISBN 0-7863-0162-7

Negotiating for Business Results
ISBN 0-7863-0114-7

Practical Business Communication
ISBN 0-7863-0227-5

High Performance Speaking
ISBN 0-7863-0222-4

Delegation Skills
ISBN 0-7863-0105-9

Coaching Skills: A Guide for Supervisors
ISBN 0-7863-0220-8

Customer Service and the Telephone
ISBN 0-7863-0224-0

Creativity at Work
ISBN   0-7863-0223-2

Effective Interpersonal Relationships
ISBN   0-7863-0255-0

The Participative Leader
ISBN   0-7863-0252-6

Building Customer Loyalty
ISBN   0-7863-0253-4

Getting and Staying Organized
ISBN   0-7863-0254-2

Total Quality Selling
ISBN   0-7863-0324-7

Business Etiquette
ISBN   0-7863-0323-9

Empowering Employees
ISBN   0-7863-0314-X

Training Skills for Supervisors
ISBN   0-7863-0313-1

Moving Meetings
ISBN   0-7863-0333-6

Multicultural Customer Service
ISBN   0-7863-0332-8

HF
5548.8
.L684
1994

Lucas, Robert W.

Effective
    interpersonal
    relationships.

$10.00